ISBN 10: 1477641106
ISBN-13: 978-1477641101

DEDICATION

This book is dedicated to Anna Lee - my favorite toddler.

With much love, Bomb Bomb

Some horses are big.

Some horses are small.

Horses are good at running.

Horses are good at jumping,
too!

Some horses carry riders.

Some horses pull carriages.

A pony is like a horse, only smaller.

Many children ride ponies.

Some horses are one color.

Some horses are two colors.

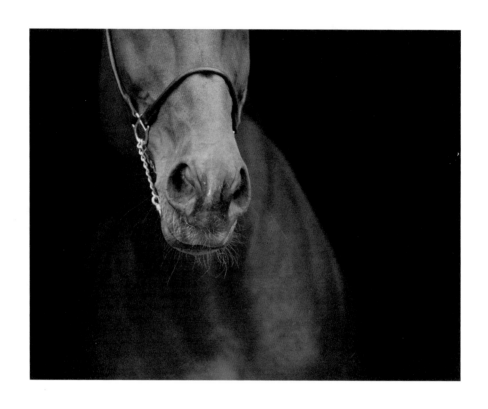

A horse's nose is called a muzzle.

A horse's foot is called a hoof.

Some horses run free and
belong to no one.

⊠

Some horses live in fences and barns and belong to people.

A mommy horse is called a
mare, and a baby horse is called
a foal.

A daddy horse is called a
stallion.

Some horses are racehorses
and run very fast.

Some horses are work horses
and are very strong.

A bridle is worn on a horse's head and helps the rider to control the horse.

A saddle is worn on a horse's back to make the rider more comfortable.

Some horses are rode with a
western-style saddle and bridle.

Some horses are rode with an English-style saddle and bridle.

A white spot on a horse's forehead is called a star.

A white streak down a horse's
nose is called a blaze.

✕✕

Some horses lie down when
they sleep.

Some horses stand when they
sleep!

A horse is tall and beautiful.

A pony is short and beautiful!

Some horses,

⊠

are made just for you!

⋈

 # The end.

We hope you enjoyed this
Curious Toddler book.

Also in the Curious Toddler series...

Let's Learn About...Dogs!
Let's Learn About...Cats!
Let's Learn About...Things to Drive!
Let's Learn About...Jungle Animals!
Let's Learn About...Birds!
Let's Learn About...Wild Animals!
Let's Learn About...Horses!
Let's Learn About...Farm Animals!

Let's Learn About ...
DOGS !
A CURIOUS TODDLER BOOK
Ages 2-5
Volume 1
Cheryl Shireman

Let's Learn About ...
CATS !
A CURIOUS TODDLER BOOK
Ages 2-5
Volume 2
Cheryl Shireman

Let's Learn About ...
Things to
DRIVE !
A CURIOUS TODDLER BOOK
Ages 2-5
Volume 3
Cheryl Shireman

Let's Learn About ...
JUNGLE ANIMALS!
A CURIOUS TODDLER BOOK
Ages 2-5
Volume 4
Cheryl Shireman

Let's Learn About ...
BIRDS!
A CURIOUS TODDLER BOOK
Ages 2-5
Volume 5
Cheryl Shireman

Let's Learn About ...
WILD ANIMALS!
A CURIOUS TODDLER BOOK
Ages 2-5
Volume 6
Cheryl Shireman

Let's Learn About ...
HORSES!
A CURIOUS TODDLER BOOK
Ages 2-5
Volume 7
Cheryl Shireman

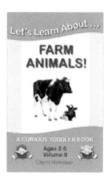

Let's Learn About ...
FARM ANIMALS!
A CURIOUS TODDLER BOOK
Ages 2-5
Volume 8
Cheryl Shireman

ABOUT THE AUTHOR

Cheryl Shireman created the Curious Toddler Series. Cheryl is married and lives in Indiana on a beautiful lake with her husband. She has three grown children and one adorable granddaughter.

Cheryl also writes novels for big people:
Life is But a Dream: On The Lake
Life is But a Dream: In The Mountains
Broken Resolutions
Cooper Moon: The Calling

She is also the author of the beloved non-fiction book, You Don't Need a Prince: A Letter to My Daughter

All of her books can be found online on Amazon.
amazon.com/author/cherylshireman
Her website is www.cherylshireman.com
She can also be found on Twitter and Facebook.

Made in the USA
Lexington, KY
06 December 2012